The Clan

The Gordons

Miles Kerr-Peterson
St Kilda Publications

St Kilda Publications
A trading division of St Kilda (Holdings) Ltd.
stkildapublications.com

45 Grovepark Street
Glasgow
G20 7NZ

First Edition 2019

ISBN: 978-1-9997567-1-0

All content © St Kilda (Holdings) Ltd. 2019
unless otherwise stated.

For more on the clans and kindreds of Scotland, visit clancentral.co.uk
Also see Romilly Squire and George Way of Plean, *The Scottish Clan & Family Encyclopaedia*, third edition (2017)

Every effort is made to make this short book as accurate as possible, with sources given in the bibliography at the back. Should you notice any major errors please contact clans@clancentral.co.uk and, where appropriate, we will update future editions.

Please note that all Clan Crest images contained on and in this book are strictly the copyright of St Kilda (holdings) Ltd. and not in the public domain. While the blazon of a clan crest can be rendered by anyone, the artistic representation of the clan crests herein were drawn for us by the renowned heraldic authority Romilly Squire and may not be reproduced without permission.

THE GORDONS IN BRIEF

Name Meaning: (lords of) the 'muddy hill' or 'spacious fort'.

Closely related kingroups ('septs'): Aitkins, Barrie, Connor, Cullen, Adie, Esslemont, Huntley, Jupp, Milne, Todd; their spelling variations, and others.

Origins: First Mentioned circa 1171 AD. Uncertain origins, but the original line of Gordons from the Merse in Berwickshire are likely to descend from the Anglo-Saxon/Anglo-Danish Northumbrian Lords of Bamburgh. From 1408 the main Gordon line was taken over by the Setons, who descend from the Normans.

Mottos: Bydand (old Scots for 'Abiding' or 'Steadfast', from the word 'bide'). Chief's motto: Animo non Astutia (Latin for 'by spirit, not cunning').

Crest (see cover): Issuant from a crest coronet Or, a stag's head (affrontée) Proper, attired with ten tines Or.

Chief's arms: (historically) three boars' heads couped Or, armed Proper, langued Gules.

INTRODUCTION
CLANS AND KINDREDS

The Gordons' power straddled both Lowlands and Highlands, although they were primarily Lowland in cultural outlook. Before we can understand their history, we should first look into the deeper history and society of old Scotland.

THE ORIGINS OF SCOTLAND

Scotland was formed from several older kingdoms and many peoples, who, over time, came to recognise the supremacy of the Kings of Scots, or were conquered by them. Originally, the term Scot was used by the Romans to refer to anyone who spoke Gaelic, and was used more for referring to the people of Ireland, as most of mainland Scotland still spoke variations of Byrthonic (which survives today in Welsh, Cornish and Bretton). Only over time did the name come to refer to a people, and those were the Gaelic speaking people of the west of what is now Scotland, and their kings.

If we start in the eighth century, in the west were the Scots, the Gaelic-speaking people whose kingdom of Dál Riata spanned Argyll, the Isles and parts of

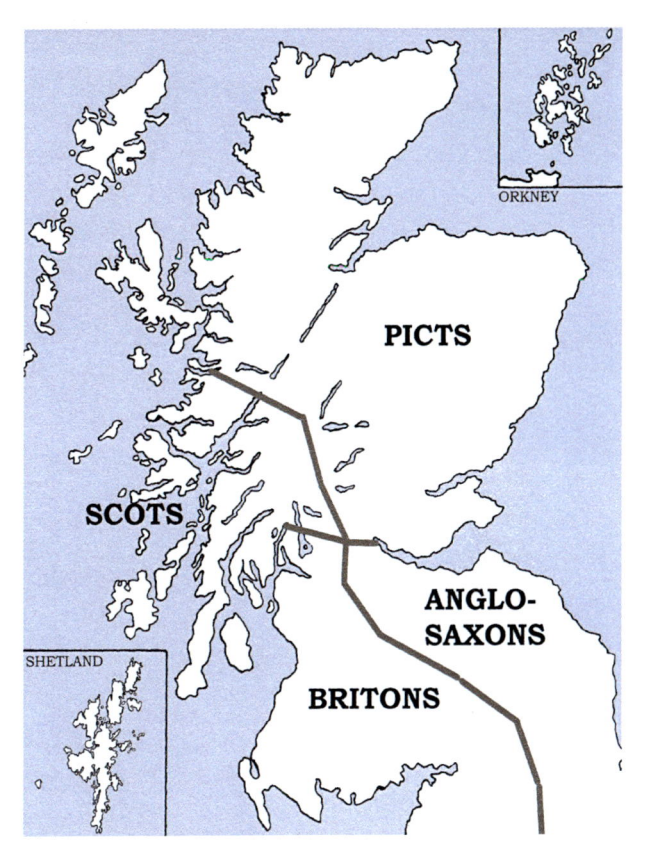

A much simplified map of the peoples of Scotland before the arrival of the Vikings in the eigth century. There was much mixing of peoples though, which means placenames of all these languages appear all over Scotland. The Gordons probably originated in the Anglo-Saxon kingdom of Bernicia.

Northern Ireland. In the east were the Picts, a series of kingdoms and provinces stretching from Caithness to the Firth of Forth. The Picts were a distinct group of Britons who had not been conquered by the Romans and had a strong and mesmerising visual culture. In the south west were the Britons in the kingdom of Strathclyde, which, at one time, stretched far to the south to include parts of modern Cumbria. They spoke an old form of Cumbric and identified closely with the southern Britons, who later became known as the Welsh. In the south east, below the Firth of Forth, focused on what is now Edinburgh, were the Anglo-Saxons of the kingdom of Bernicia, who spoke Old English. These divisions and borders changed often, and in the ninth century Danish and Norse invaders, the Vikings, arrived and conquered the Isles and devastated the existing kingdoms. They established two more kingdoms, that of the Isles and another in Galloway.

Under the Scottish king Kenneth MacAlpin the Scots and Picts merged into one unified kingdom. Over the following centuries the new kingdom conquered and incorporated parts of the Anglo-Saxon, British and Viking territories to form the kingdom we recognise today. Norman knights were also invited to live in Scotland by a series of kings.

Over time the old distinctions fell away until there was one identity, the Scots, although with two major cultural regions, the Highlands (including the Isles) and the Lowlands.

HIGHLANDS AND LOWLANDS

The most fundamental and obvious difference between Highland and Lowland is simple geography. One is high and mountainous, the other is low lying. However, the difference runs much deeper and has three main strands: language, culture and economy.

As Scotland formed, the old Pictish language (probably a distant variation of Brythonic) was supplanted by Gaelic. The Brythonic-Cumbric language of Strathclyde withered away. This left Gaelic and the Old English of the south east, which gradually developed into a separate language, that of Scots. Scots was adopted at the Scottish court in the thirteenth century and by the fifteenth century had become dominant throughout the Lowlands. The Highlands kept Gaelic, where it is still spoken in areas to this day, as did the south west, at least until the end of the sixteenth century. From its zenith as the language of court and most of Scotland in the eleventh century, Gaelic was increasingly marginalised and the last known Scottish monarch to speak the language was James IV (1473-1513). The language continued to flourish in the Highlands, however, where traditional household courts and bards kept the it alive.

Culturally, the Highlands and Lowlands differed in their outlook. The Highlands had a strong identity through their language and tended to look towards Gaelic Ireland. The Lowlands were more subject to the European fashions of their day: strong diplomatic and trading links kept the Lowlanders especially abreast of developments on the Continent, particularly the Baltic, the Low Countries and in France. Economically, Highlands and Lowlands were perhaps the most different. The Highlands relied on fishing, cattle and subsistence farming, whereas the Lowlands had a fuller agricultural and trading economy, flourishing with towns, markets and ocean going harbours.

These broad differences between Highland and Lowland run deeper than mere geography, and hence, for example, parts of Aberdeenshire are certainly upland and geographically Highland, yet were more culturally related to the Lowlands. There are many exceptions to this simplified Highland and Lowland divide, such as the Northern Isles (Orkney and Shetland), which had a distinctly Scandinavian dialect and cultural outlook, which came from the Norse connections established there during the age of Viking conquest. Galloway and the Borders also mark to further distinct regions within the kingdom - Scotland has always been a very diverse country.

THE LOWLANDS
THE KINDRED AND SURNAME

In the Lowlands, 'Clans' are best thought of as 'Kindreds', but - either way - they emerged as units in the twelfth and thirteenth centuries. This was when the ancient family and power structures of Scotland met with new European notions of lordship and what has been called a 'feudal' structure of society. As such, most of the famous clans and kindreds were formed between 1150 and 1350, although often with older pedigrees for the chiefly line. Clans and Kindreds may have been blood-family units at their core, but they fitted into a wider and hierarchical system of lordship, at the top of which was the king. In other words, the chiefs' power over their clans came from their ability to lead their family and other smaller families. This was combined with their power over land, which came from the Crown, or some more powerful lord. These lands then supported the clan and their dependents, thus making a circle of power. This was the essence of clanship. Clans could have Scottish, Cumbric, Norse, Irish, English, Norman or Flemish origins: all found their place and thrived in Scotland and adapted into Scottish society.

This structure of 'clanship' was more or less universal throughout Scotland (albeit with different names and emphases) until Highland and Lowland started to substantially differ after about 1500. However, the notion that Highland clanship was any different to Lowland kinship only emerged after about 1600. Clanship in the Highlands survived into the eighteenth century when it was dramatically and traumatically terminated after the Jacobite rebelions, whereas in the Lowlands it petered out gradually over the seventeenth century - mainly because other institutions started serving the protective and social roles of the clan/kindred - such as the Kirk or the law courts.

Kinship was the fundamental building block of a society in which loyalty to blood relatives represented the most basic social obligation. The extended kingroup was usually recognised and identified by surname, and the reference point was a common ancestor from whom everyone knew their relationship. Some kingroups were huge: the Gordons, for example, dominated the north east of Scotland and had some 150 kin branches, their head being the Earl of Huntly. The Keiths by contrast, headed by the Earl Marischal, had only 11 major kin branches. Each kingroup would usually have a recognised head, the representative of the 'main line', who was the closest male descendant of the common ancestor in the rules of primogeniture (where the eldest son inherited all). The Arbuthnots, a modest but prosperous family in Kincardineshire, for example, would look to the Arbuthnot Lairds of Arbuthnot (known as Arbuthnot 'of that ilk' when the family name was the same as the place name), in succession, from father to eldest son.

Kinship was a universal tie between individuals, be they labourer, laird or noble; each in theory had their own recognised responsibilities and obligations to each other, depending on their position within the kingroup. Surnames (almost universal in the Lowlands by 1500) were such a strong identifier of a person's connections and such a powerful notion for the early modern Scot, that the word 'surname' was often used as a byword for 'kindred', or the Highland word 'clan'. Of course, this was very much an ideal of social relations: it is questionable, for example, over time and over long distances how much obligation a person would actually feel towards a complete stranger merely because they shared the same surname. However, where the common identity of a kingroup was reinforced by personal connections and geographical proximity, its force in medieval and early modern Scotland represented a very strong binding glue for society. The obligations of kinship were certainly stronger in Scotland for longer than in most contemporary European countries.

The emphasis of kinship was usually centred on male ancestry. For example, if your father was a Kennedy and your mother a Douglas, you were primarily aligned with the Kennedys. Legally, women were then added to or subtracted from kingroups, leaving one family to join another at the point of marriage. Socially, however, things were much more fluid, since marriage could bring kingroups into alliance and women usually retained strong connections to their original families. Wives even retaining their original surnames after they married and this practice only started to die out in the eighteenth century. Hence the children of unions could identify with their mother's families as much as with their father's surname. Therefore the concept of 'family', 'clan' and 'kindred' could reach far beyond those bearing the same name.

LORDSHIP

For a European kingdom, late medieval and early modern Scotland was an unusually localised and de-centralised country. Power was mostly exercised personally, not administratively, and people owed allegiance to their king and their lord (often referred to nowadays as a 'chief'). The government and its advisors were distant, occasionally a nuisance, but mostly abstract. At its most basic level society was a relationship between lord and man. Ideally this system worked on two principles; paternalism and protection. The lord gave land and offered protection. His men worked the land and offered fees, rents and military service. Men who wished to follow a particular lord offered a written or verbal bond of manrent, which promised to serve his lord, give advice and accompany him. Lords had the right to call their dependents and tenants for a range of services, including military service when required (although the need declined over time), but the lords were also responsible in law for their men, dependants and tenants. This was an intensely hierarchical society.

The kingroups fitted into this larger system of lordship. Usually the man bonding himself to a lord would be the head of a smaller kingroup and so lesser families became bound to greater ones: the Buchanan kindred, for example, recognised the Stewart Earls of Lennox as their superiors. Often this relationship worked within the same kingroup, lesser cadet branches of a family would serve the main line. Hence the Keith Lairds of Ravenscraig held the castle and lands of the same name from the Keith Earls Marischal. These lairds managed the earldom's lands in Buchan, while the earls defended the family's interests from rival lords.

There has been a misrepresentative image of the greater Scottish nobleman as violent, unruly and over-mighty. They are often seen as having only been interested in greedily serving their own selfish ends and were happy to kill each other and their kings (James I and James III), even being responsible for forcing Mary Queen of Scots to abdicate in 1567. Although there are certainly instances of this: the sixth Earl of Huntly famously murdered the second ('the bonny') Earl of Moray in 1592; Robert and Patrick Stewart, first and second Earls of Orkney, exercised brutally repressive lordships in the Northern Isles until the latter's execution for treason in 1614. Yet such men were the exception, and the reality was much more nuanced. Lords could not be pantomime villains if they wanted to survive and prosper; their position depended on the advice, support and consent of their supporters and inferiors. Power was contractual and (ideally at least) mutually beneficial. Lordship was, of course, open to damning abuse at times, but a good lord knew that it was a reciprocal relationship and it was in his interests to keep his followers maintained and content, as that was the foundation of his power.

The reciprocal nature of society bound Scotland tightly and meant that it was relatively cohesive. Compared to many European neighbours, there were far fewer instances of popular protest and peasant revolts. The personal nature of lordship gave opportunities to vent grievances and the connections between those at the bottom and those at the top provided enough contact in which troubles could be worked through. More major problems could be resolved through resorting to the law, the Kirk, or other outside mediation. Scotland seems to have had relatively good social cohesion compared to either France or England. Of course there were tensions and problems: there were urban and religious riots, or skirmishes and brawls between enemies, but there is a certain lack of violence based around lordship. There was nothing similar, for example, to the enclosure riots of England or the peasant rebellions of France, at least until 1724 with the Galloway Levellers movement in south west Scotland. These men rose against enclosure of land previously used for crops for the pasturing of cattle, which had put them out of work. By that time the old system of lordship had broken down anyway, leaving 'landlordism', a mere economic exchange, in its place. This is not to say that Scotland was some sort of utopia, far from it - there were still many problems and injustices - but it at least seemed to work most of the time.

Did this system of kinship and lordship lead to institutionalised corruption? Yes. Did they lead to abuses of power? Certainly. But as everyone was bound up within the one system contemporaries expected these downsides, it was just the way the world worked. People did not stand equal in the sight of the law, because they were not individuals; they were only small elements of larger group power and the nobles were the physical manifestations of this. Families and lordships acted together as one body, everyone was connected to everyone else in some immediate way.

BLOODFEUD

One of the side effects of this system of kinship and lordship was the bloodfeud. At its most basic level the system worked on the principle of mutually assured destruction. Because everyone was linked and mutually dependent on everyone else, disputes between individuals became disputes between kingroups and so between lordships. Disputes which spilled into violence would lead to retaliation and further violence, drawing in more and more people. The vertical ties which bound all layers of society meant that when fighting broke out at one point, then it could easily ascend or descend, unless intervention was taken. Some feuds could run over large territories and across generations, such as those between the Gordons and the Moray Stewarts in the North, or the Kerrs and the Scotts in the borders.

Perversely, it was this very principle of violence which led to an aversion to bloodshed and a major incentive to stop any dispute escalating out of control. Few would want to follow a dispute through to its logical conclusion In theory, everyone knew the rules; everyone knew the process of mediation and the appropriate forms of settlement and compensation. This was an imperfect system; it kept the peace most of the time, but it did occasionally break down. Yet the famous cases are the rare ones, most disputes could be amicably settled through kin, friends and without recourse to outside and governmental intervention. The fear of the descent into mutually assured bloody destruction usually ensured this.

LOWLAND WOMEN

As with the rest of European society at the time, the women of Scotland were not treated equally to men. Women were directly excluded from politics and church government; as girls they were dependant on their fathers, as women they were dependant on their husbands. Their husbands were usually chosen by their fathers as a matter of policy. Marriage was an important part of a kingroup's wider strategy, through the need for dynastic alliances, to advance lineages, and the preservation of property within a family. These pressures combined to influence any marriage choice, rather than any notion of love or companionship. That said, however, Scottish law required marriage to only need the consent of the individuals involved, paternal consent was desirable but not essential, which gave many women a degree of additional freedom. Yet despite these constraints, in some ways the lot of a Scotswoman was marginally better than her counterparts elsewhere in Britain or on the Continent. Although legally women were little better than minors, this was slightly better than some parts of Europe, where they were little better than property.

The Gordons

ORIGIN LEGENDS

We need to deal with a few myths and legends before we move to the actual history of the Gordons. The first is that the Gordons come from the ancient Macedonian city of Gordonia, then travelled through Gaul, before coming to Scotland. This is simply a case of linking various unrelated but similar sounding placenames and making a story out of them, which was an especially popular method of doing history in the later middle ages. Next is that the Gordons came from France and are descended from the Duke of Gordoune, who was constable to the mighty king Charlemagne in the year 800. Again, this is joining the dots, the Scottish Gordons derive their name from a Scottish placename, while the French, and other like-named English families, derive their similar names from similar sounding, but different, placenames.

The Scottish Gordons are unrelated to the southern English surnames of Gurdon or Gordun, which historians assume to derive from either Adam de Gurdun (Adam of Gurdun), mentioned in Hampshire in 1204, whose name probably refers to one of the many French 'Gordon' style placenames, or the likes of Geoffry Gurdun, mentioned in Kent in 1220, or Adam Gordon mentioned in 1279 in Cambridgeshire. Their names are assumed to come from the French surname Gourdon, which is based on a word for dull or stupid. Note that before the late nineteenth century, spellings weren't standardised, meaning that all the Scottish, French and English 'Gordons' spelt their name in many different ways (often in the same documents), meaning exact modern spelling doesn't really help in identifying where the name originates.

Finally there are a couple of stories of Gordons during the reign of Malcolm III, and specifically the year 1093. One tells of a Gordon who accompanied the king during a raid into Northumbria, the second that a Richard Gordon slew a monstrous animal in the Merse and was hence granted lands. Neither story can be substantiated by contemporary records, and this was the age before surnames had developed. The monster story was probably invented to explain the three boars' heads on the Gordon coat of arms, although these were more likely to have been borrowed from the related Swinton family. It's not until 1171 that we get a firm historical reference to the first Gordon in Scottish history. These stories may have a grain of truth to them, perhaps garbled family stories passed down and corrupted over the years, but we shouldn't give them too much credence.

Above: a rendering of the early arms of the chiefly Gordon line, likely borrowed from the Swintons.
Below: Bamburgh Castle, possible seat of the Gordon ancestors.

ORIGINS

The Gordons first emerge in the historical record in 1171. The Gordon surname is derived from the man who held the lands of Gordon, which lies in the Merse and is close to the border with England, not far from Lauder, Hume, Kelso and Colstream. The exact origin of the placename Gordon is uncertain; it has been argued that it might be Old English 'Gor-doun' meaning 'mud hill' or Old Welsh 'Gor-din' meaning 'spacious fort'. Given the possible Anglo-Saxon origins of the family, discussed below, the former may be more likely.

The Gordons seem to have been closely related to the once powerful Swinton family, who held the lands of the same name not far from Gordon. The two families had identical arms of three boars' heads, and given their proximity, this suggests a family relationship, otherwise we would expect completely different arms to actually help identify who was who. The boars' heads make the most heraldic sense with the Swinton name 'Swine Farmstead' for obvious reasons. The Swintons seem to have been a more important family than the Gordons, at least before the Wars of Independence, and it is thus not impossible to suspect that the Gordons descend from a younger son of the Swintons.

The lands held by the Gordons and the Swintons in the 1100s were probably territories bought into the Scottish kingdom by the Earls of Dunbar, who had been Anglo-Saxon-Danish lords of Northumbria. These lords were forced to abandon their territories south of the Tweed at the time of the Norman Conquest of England following 1066. Richard Gordon and Sir Adam Gordon were witnesses to a charter of Patrick, Earl of Dunbar, made sometime between 1182 and 1189 for the lands of Swinton, and there may have been some link between the early Gordons and the household of the earls. In later documents the earls are described as the superiors of the Gordon lands.

The Swintons claim descent from the Anglo-Danish lord, Waltheof of Bamburgh (active in the 990s and ancestor of the Earls of Dunbar). The territorial location of the first Gordons, thier lordly connections to the earls, and the possible connections to the Swintons all hint towards a Northumbrian heritage of the family - referring to the former Anglo-Saxon and later Anglo-Danish kingdom that stretched at one time from the Firth of Forth to the Humber (not the modern county). We cannot be wholly certain of this, but it makes some sense given the circumstantial evidence.

THE FIRST GORDON: RICHARD 'RICHER' DE GORDON
Active c.1171-1199

This man is often referred to as RICHER, as that is how his name was spelt in a charter belonging to the Abbey of Kelso. This is a handy way to distinguish him from other Richard Gordons, although not too much emphasis should be placed on the spelling of names at this time.

Richer is mentioned in a charter (basically a receipt for a land transaction) of 1171, when he granted a small collection of lands to the parish church in Gordon and Kelso Abbey. These lands including the 'whole land of the burial ground', and the significance of this is a little puzzling. It might suggest that Richer or his predecessors had initially founded and endowed the church on their land and then gifted them to the keeping of Kelso. It was common at this time for landowners to gift lands and properties to abbeys and monasteries in return for prayers and masses for their eternal souls. Gifting the burial ground, which was land of little economic benefit in itself and presumably attached to the church anyway, may have been part of completing the process of the foundation.

The ruins of Kelso Abbey

The only other mention of Richer (spelt this time as Ricard de Gordun) is as witness to a charter of Patrick, Earl of Dunbar, gifting lands at Swinton to Saint Cuthbert (represented by Durham Cathedral). We do not know when this charter was made, but we know the earl died around 1232, so it must pre-date that. Also mentioned in the list of witnesses is Alan, son of Cospatric of Swinton, again hinting at the associations between the Gordons, the Swintons and the Dunbars.

Also a mentioned in this document are two more Gordons. Sir Adam de Gordon is the first, and he is described as son of the Adam de Gordon, the second mentioned. These men held the lands of Easter Gordon, a smaller part of the larger Gordon lands. Presumably these two lines of 'de Gordons' were related branches of the same family, the Easter Gordons being from a younger brother of an unnamed ancestor, and given a hived-off western part of the Gordon lands to sustain themselves.

That is all that is known about Richer, the first Gordon in Scottish history. As lord of the lands of Gordon it is possible he was buried in the parish church there, although he may instead have been buried at the higher-status Kelso Abbey, to whom he had made hearty gifts.

GORDON CASTLE
Gordon Seat from at least 1171 to 1580

The original home of the Gordons in Berwickshire, home to Richer and his successors, is now lost and forgotten. There are two candidates for its location.

To the north of the settlement of Gordon are some fields called 'Castle Parks', nearby there are the traces of an oval enclosure, which might indicates the site of a fort. The other candidate is the site of Greenknowe Tower, to the west of Gordon. The ancestral lands of Gordon passed out of the Gordon hands in 1580, coming to Sir James Seton, and Seton appears to have made his residence at Greenknowe, inscribing the date of his ownership, 1581, on a lintel over the entrance. The site of Greenknowe (meaning 'green hill') is quite defensible, being surrounded by marshland. It is quite possible that Seton remodelled a much older Gordon home, rather than building something new on an unused site.

It may be that the northern fort was home of the original line of Gordons, while Greenknowe was the seat of the Easter Gordons, who took over the leadership of the family after only a couple of generations.

Greenknowe Tower mostly dates to the sixteenth century, but probably occupies the site of either the original castle of Gordon or Easter Gordon.

St Michael's Church, Gordon, Berwickshire

Nothing survives of the original church at Gordon. It would have been an important place for the first Gordons, and may also have been their burial place.

A 1906 Ordinance Survey Map of Gordon, showing the church, Greenknowe Tower and the assumed site of Gordon Castle to the north.

SUCCESSION OF THE GORDONS OF GORDON

Richer de Gordon - active c.1171-1199

Sir Thomas de Gordon (I) active c.1220s, confirmed his father's gifts to Kelso, but also made his own gifts to the nuns of Coldstream. Little evidence about this man survives, although he was clearly prosperous enough to generously give livestock (sheep, pigs and cattle) to the nuns.

Sir Thomas de Gordon (II) active c.1232-1258, also gave generously to Kelso and Coldstream. We learn that his wife was called Marjorie, who is the first recorded woman of the family - although we do not know which family she had came from.

Alicia / Alice de Gordon active c.1258, Thomas and Marjorie had no male children, so the succession passed to their daughter, Alice. When we first have mention of her, she is described as heir to Sir Thomas and a widow of Adam de Gordon, when she confirmed all the gifts she had made to Kelso. This Adam Gordon was from the Gordons of Wester Gordon, to whom the succession of the chiefly line now passed.

THE GORDONS OF WESTER GORDON

This branch of the Gordons held the lands of Easter Gordon, adjoining Richer's lands. Presumably the Wester Gordons were a younger cadet branch of the Gordons, Adam I possibly being brother to Richer.

Adam de Gordon (I) active c.1182, is mentioned as father of Sir Adam de Gordon, sometime between 1182 and 1199. Adam I is noted as a witness in some charters relating to Thomas de Gordon, dating to between 1219 and 1221.

Sir Adam de Gordon (II) active c.1180s-1240s, appears in a charter, dating to sometime between 1182 and 1199, as a witness alongside Richer de Gordon, the first recorded Scottish Gordon mentioned above. In another charter relating to Thomas de Gordon, both Adam and his father were witnesses, alongside the Earl of Dunbar. Sir Adam gifted some of his lucrative peat lands in Fans to Dryburgh Abbey, for the benefit of his soul and that of his wife, Alice (probaby daughter of Sir Thomas). In another chater he gave some land within Easter Gordon to Melrose Abbey, this time for the benefit of himself, his ancestors and his successors. This charter also mentions his son John, and his steward, Patrick.

Sir Adam Gordon (III) active 1296-1309, is first mentioned in 1296 submitting to King Edward I in the Ragman Roll. Edward had just invaded Scotland and crushed all opposition, deposed King John, effectively extinguishing Scotland as an independent kingdom. In the face of such might most Scottish nobles had little option but to submit, and Gordon's lands were directly in the English warpath.

Legends suggest that Sir Adam fought alongside William Wallace, although this looks to have been wishful thinking on the part of later generations, as most families sought to re-write their stories after the messy Wars of Independence. Instead, Sir Adam seems to have kept his allegiance to the English, being sent by them at one point as an envoy to France. He served them as Justicar of Lothian and even held the Castle of Inverkip (Ardgowan in Renfrewshire) for the English Crown.

By the 1310s Adam's relationship to the English invaders had soured, as his lands were being raided by both Scots and English. He seems to have come over to the forces of Robert the Bruce either just before or just after the Battle of Bannockburn in 1314. King Robert was good to his new follower, granting him the lands of Stichel in Roxburghshire in 1315. From being a lukewarm adherent

The Scottish counter-copy of the Declaration of Arbroath, the letter to the Pope asserting Scotland's independence. The copy that Sir Adam took to Avignon has hence been lost. The Declaration was part of Bruce's wider campaign to secure his grip on the kingship and to reject the claim of the English kings to overlordship of Scotland.

to the Scottish cause he came to be one of Bruce's most trusted men: Sir Adam had the great honour to serve as the ambassador to Pope John XXII in 1320, delivering the famous Declaration of Arbroath. This Latin-language document asserted Scottish Independence and resistance to the English King. After some fairly eccentric pseudo history about the Scots originally coming from Scythia (now in modern Iran), it asserts: 'it is, in truth, not for glory, riches nor honours that we fight, but for freedom alone, which no honest man gives up but with life itself'

In reward for his service Sir Adam was granted the lands of Strathbogie in Aberdeenshire. This was a momentous moment for the Gordons, shifting their focus from the Borderlands to the North, turning a fairly unremarkable knightly family into some of the premier lords in the kingdom. Before he died, Sir Adam continued the fight against his former paymasters, leading an attack accross the border on Norham Castle, although his forces were defeated and driven back across the Tweed. Sir Adam was married to a woman called Amabilla, although we know little about her or even from which family she came from. They had several children, and their second son, William, is ancestor to the **Gordons of Lochinvar and Kenmure** in Dumfries and Galloway.

STRATHBOGIE/HUNTLY CASTLE

The Castle of Strathbogie was later renamed Huntly after Gordon lands of the same name in Berwickshire. The Gordons built a new stone castle on an older twelfth-century Motte and Bailey. The mound of the old great motte survives today, although only the foundations of the original Gordon-built tower can be seen below this.

The castle was burnt in 1452 by the Douglases under the Earl of Moray, and rebuilt grander than it was before - after the Douglases had been revenged, of course. Over the decades the Gordons built more and more on to their great castle, although it was fired again by King James VI in 1589, when the oldest part, the great stone tower, was blown up by gunpowder. The Gordons rebuilt again, creating a spectacular Renaissance Palace, including grand fireplaces, turrets and a stunning heraldic doorway. This doorway depicted the arms of the Earl of Huntly, above which were the arms of the King of Scotland, then above that was the 'Arma Christi' the Arms of Jesus Christ, then above that a sunburst showing the Archangel Michael; when you visit and go through this door, you're supposed to be reminded that you're at the bottom, with the hierarchy (and hospitality) of lordship and the heavens above you. This was a strong statement of the

Huntly Castle, from Billings' Baronial and Ecclesiastical Antiquities of Scotland *(1845-52)*

family's Roman Catholicism (Scotland having turned Protestant by this point) and was so controvercial that part of it was forcibly removed in the 1640s.

Sadly, Huntly Castle was again sacked during the Wars of the Three Kingdoms in the 1640s. This time there was no revivial, and after the wars the great palace gradually fell to ruin, leaving the shell as we see it today.

Huntly Castle's great heraldic portal.

Sir Adam Gordon (IV), active 1314-1351, fought as one of the leaders of the Scottish forces at the Battle of Halidon Hill in 1333, when Scottish troops were heavily defeated by the English King Edward III. Sir Adam seems to have survived at least. He died at roughly the same time as the Black Death was ravaging Scotland, although the exact cause of his demise is unrecorded.

John Gordon (I), active 1357-1361, seems to have served among the great number of Scottish forces fighting for the French in the Hundred Years War against the English, and was captured for a time. His wife was called Elizabeth. So many Scots were said to have taken the opportunity to fight for the French that Henry V is said to have remarked that no English king invaded France without finding Scots in his path.

Sir John Gordon (II), active 1376-1395, saw as much military action as his predecessors, fighting at the Battles of Carham, Melrose and Otterburn. Sir John had no legitimate children, so his brother Adam inheirited. John had two illigitmate children though, John (or 'Jock') of Essie and Thomas ('Tam') of Ruthven. Out of these two illigitmate Gordons spring a staggering one-hundred-and-twenty-two branches of the extended Gordon kindred.

Jock's eldest son was Alexander and from his sons come the **Gordons of Buckie, Deskie, Tulloch** and many others. From his second son John come the **Gordons of Balbithan, Cairnborrow, Lungar Drumwhindle, Glenbucket, Kindrocht, Pitlurg** and others.

From Jock's second son William come the **Gordons of Balmad, Buthlaw, Craig, Crichie, Knock, Lesmoir, Merdrum, Tilyangus** and others. From Jock's third son James come the **Gordons of Balmuir, Bonnyton** (in Ayrshire), **Haddo, Methlick, Scotstown** (in Renfrewshire) and others.

From Tam's sixteen sons come the **Gordons of Balveny, Clunymore, Noth** and many others.

Sir Adam Gordon (V), active 1398-1402, is famous for an incident at the Battle of Homildon in 1402 (which is described by Walter Bower, Shakespeare and Sir Walter Scott). The Gordons had fallen into feud with their old neighbours and probable kinsmen, the Swintons. Despite this, as the battle against the English began, Gordon sprang from his horse and, kneeling, begged the superior Swinton for forgiveness and to be knighted by his hand. Now, as friends, they then charged side by side towards the enemy at the head of a hundred cavalry. Their charge stunned the English, but both were killed in the fierce fighting. His wife was Elizabeth Keith.

A spirited Victorian depiction of Gordon and Swinton charging at Homildon in 1402.

John Gordon (III), active 1406-1408, is almost unknown to history, leaving next to no imprint in the written records. He had no children, so was succeeded by his sister. With John the direct line of the Gordons of Easter Gordon died.

THE SETON-GORDONS

Elizabeth Gordon, active 1407-1439, was sister to John and she married Alexander Seton, second son of Sir William Seton of that Ilk. The Setons were Anglo-Normans who seem to have been in Scotland since about the time of Malcolm III (1058-1093). Elizabeth did not have much choice in the match, as she was unmarried when she succeeded her father. Her 'ward', the right of a man to act as her guardian, was sold by the Regent, Robert, Duke of Albany, to Walter Haliburton of Direlton, who then sold it again to Sir William Seton, who then took the opportunity to marry his second son to this wealthy heiress. Alexander became Lord of Gordon, and fought at the bloody Battle of Harlaw in 1411, on the royalist side, and was knighted soon afterwards. Seton died in the winter of 1440, a year or so after Elizabeth. Their second son, William, is ancestor of the Setons of Meldrum.

Sir Alexander Seton (II), active 1427-1470, was made **first Earl of Huntly** in 1445 and appointed the king's Lieutenant of the North, an office the earls would hold for several generations. As lieutenant he confronted the rebellious Earl of Crawford at the Battle of Brechin in 1452, where Huntly was victorious. That year he also

The tomb of Sir Alexander Seton/Gordon, first Earl of Huntly, in Elgin Cathedral, where many Gordons are buried.

came into conflict with the Douglases, who burnt Strathbogie before they too were crushed. In the later part of this decade Alexander changed his surname to Gordon. Alexander witnessed James II being killed by an exploding cannon at Roxburgh in 1460. He lived for another ten years and was buried in Elgin Cathedral, where his successors established a burial aisle. His tomb is still there. Alexander had married Egidia Hay in 1427, who was from another powerful northern family, then after her death he married Elizabeth Crichton in 1440. Alexander's sons split their inheiritance. His eldest son, Alexander (who retained the name Seton) took his mother's estates and became the ancestor of the Setons of Touch and the Maxwell-Setons. The second son, George Gordon, became second Earl of Huntly. Alexander and Elizabeth's third son Adam Gordon, who was Dean of Caithness, is ancestor to the **Gordons of Beldornie, Wardhouse, Embo, Invergordon, Ardoch, Carroll** and others.

George Gordon, second Earl of Huntly, active 1441-1501. After the fall of the Douglases, the power of the Gordons grew unchallenged. Their control over their lands was almost regal, and the chiefs are still referred to as 'Cock o' the North'. The second earl was a close associate of James III and, as his Lieutenant of the

North, led the king's forces against the rebellious Earl of Ross and forced the errant nobleman to seek peace. Huntly remained loyal to James III until the king was deposed in 1488. Huntly was eventually won over by James IV and served him as chancellor.

In 1496 Huntly Castle hosted the marriage of the pretender to the English throne, Perkin Warbeck, believed at the time to be one of the missing sons of Edward IV (the 'princes in the tower'). Warbeck was married to Huntly's daughter, Lady Catherine Gordon. James IV honoured the couple with his presence, although he was a frequent visitor to Strathbogie anyway. Warbeck invaded the south of England, but was soundly defeated at Exeter by Henry VII. Catherine was captured at St Michael's Mount in Cornwall. Although she was initially a prisoner of the English king, she went on to have a remarkable life, becoming a favourite lady-in-waiting to Henry's wife Elizabeth of York. She married three more times, built a career at court and acquired English lands. She spent most of her life at Fyfield Manor in Berkshire (which survives to this day) and was buried in the nearby church when she died. An effigy of her could be seen in St Mary's Church in Swansea, erected by her third husband, although it was destroyed during the Second World War.

Alexander Gordon, third Earl of Huntly, active 1485-1524, was Catherine's brother, and, like the second earl, enjoyed a close relationship with King James IV, helping his king subdue the Western Isles. Alexander was lucky to survive the disastrous Battle of Flodden, unlike the king. He died in 1524. From Alexander's brother, James, descend the **Gordons of Gight.** From Alexander's second son, Alexander, descend the **Gordons of Cluny**. The first son, John, died in 1517, and it was his son, George, who succeeded as fourth earl.

George, fourth Earl of Huntly, 1514-1562, became Chancellor of Scotland in 1547 and was a close confidant of the formidable regent, Mary of Guise, the mother of Mary, Queen of Scots and widow of James IV. Although the earls flirted with the new faith, the majority of the Gordons paid scant attention to the Protestant Reformation in 1560, remaining firmly Catholic. Initially Huntly enjoyed a good relationship with Queen Mary when she returned to Scotland, but they became estranged, largely a result of the influence of Mary's half-brother, James Stewart, Earl of Moray. Huntly was forced into open rebellion, but died suddenly of apoplexy while leading his men at the Battle of Corrichie. Huntly's dead body was put on trial and his son, Sir John Gordon, was later beheaded at Aberdeen.

Sir John's younger brother **George Gordon** (active from 1549-1576) was pardoned by Queen Mary and succeeded as **fifth Earl of Huntly.** Despite his father and brother's execution, George adhered to his queen as her reign went from crisis to crisis, leading to her forced abdication in 1567. George raised an army for her and marched south to fight.

George's sister Jean was a close personal friend of Queen Mary, and in 1566 was married to James Hepburn, fourth Earl of Bothwell. However, the next year they divorced, partially on the grounds that Bothwell had been sleeping with Jean's maid, but also so Bothwell would be free to woo Queen Mary. The noxious earl famously kidnapped and raped the queen, marrying her only eight days after the divorse to Jean was finalised. Later that year Bothwell was driven out of Scotland by a party of outraged fellow noblemen. He spent the best part of a decade chained to a pillar at Dragsholm Castle in Denmark, where he descended into madness and died. Jean, meanwhile, was married in 1573 to the sickly Alexander Gordon, twelfth Earl of Sutherland. As Alexander fell increasingly ill, it was left to Jean to manage and defend the earldom from Dunrobin Castle. Sutherland died in 1594, which meant Jean was able to marry again, for love this time. to Alexander Ogilvy of Boyne in 1599.

*Above, Corgarff Castle, site of Adam Gordon's massacre.
Below, George Gordon, first Marquiss of Huntly and his wife,
Henrietta Stewart, weathered carvings from Huntly Castle*

George and Jean's youngest brother was Adam Gordon of Auchindoun, known also as Edom o' Gordon. During the Civil War that erupted after the flight of Queen Mary, Adam kept control of the north while his brother the earl was in the south. Adam savagely harassed the neighbouring Forbes kindred and decisively defeated the enemies of Queen Mary at the Battle of Tillieangus. He then went on to commit one of the worst atrocities of the war, the buring of Corgarff Castle with twenty-four people inside - men, women and children, including Lady Towie and her daughters. The Marian Civil War was concluded in 1573, when Huntly recognised the infant King James VI as his monarch. Adam was sent into exile, while the earl returned north. George died suddenly in 1576 at Strathbogie, having collapsed during a game of football.

He was succeeded by his son, **George Gordon, sixth Earl of Huntly (1562-1636)**, who was one of the most remarkable and powerful men of his age. George was, despite rebelling several times against the crown, one of the closest personal friends of James VI, which gave him a large degree of immunity from his religious and political controversies. George was an agent for the Spanish Counter-Reformation in Scotland, and, like his predecessors, ruthlessly pursued his bloodfeuds.

In 1592 Huntly and his men murdered James Stewart, second Earl of Moray. The Gordons had set fire to Stewart's castle of Donibristle and Moray was forced out of his stronghold - while on fire - and, after putting up a fight, was killed. His last words were said to have been to Huntly, who had just slashed his head: 'you ha'e spoilt a far fairer face than yer ain!' Eventually, under massive political pressure, King James was forced to send his friend Huntly into exile. The Gordons eventually made peace with the crown, and in 1599 the earl was created **Marquess of Huntly**. Beside his cruel side, Huntly was also highly cultured. He was responsible for thoroughly remodelling the major Gordon castles into some of the finest renaissance palaces in Scotland, chiefly expressed in the (now mostly demolished) House of Bog/Castle Gordon and Strathbogie/Huntly Castle (now ruined).

The House of Bog was also called **Bog o' Gight** and was developed by the Gordons from about the fourteenth century, until it had become a great Renaissance Palace under the first Marquess. Great towers, turrets and chimneys decorated the skyline. Where Strathbogie was the Gordon's main powerbase, the Bog was the Gordon's more comfortable home, and they spent a great amount of time here, becoming their main house after Strathbogie fell to ruin. It was

The grand Renaissance Palace of Bog o' Gight

thoroughly rebuilt in the classical style in 1769 under the plans of architect John Baxter. A large portion of this was demolished in the 1950s.

George Gordon, second Marquess of Huntly, 1592-1649, was a fierce supporter of the royalist cause in the civil wars of the 1640s, and his followers have passed into history as the Gordon Horse, which figured prominently in the campaigns of the great Royalist general, the Marquess of Montrose. Huntly's pride was such that he found it impossible to work with Montrose, and some historians have suggested that had he done so

George Gordon, second Marquess of Huntly

with any gusto, then the whole course of the war in Scotland might have been very different. Huntly was captured at Strathdon in December 1647 and was taken to Edinburgh, where he was beheaded in 1649. He had remained steadfastly Catholic, like his predecessors. When asked by the Presbyterian ministers before the execution, whether he wanted their excommunication against him lifted, he retorted 'that as he was not accustomed to give ear to false prophets, he did not wish to be troubled by him'. The marquess' eldest son, Lord George Gordon, had been killed in 1645 at the Battle of Alford, so his younger son, Lewis, succeeded as Marquess.

Louis Gordon, third Marquess of Huntly, 1626-1653, had served with distinction throughout the Civil Wars, fighting on both sides for a time and was restored to the family estates and titles in 1651. This dashing soldier died at the age of only twenty-seven.

His son, **George Gordon, fourth Marquess of Huntly,** 1643-1716, another soldier, fought for Louis XIV of France in the 1670s. He returned to Scotland in 1675 and was known as a libertine, a fop and a Roman Catholic. He was raised to be **Duke of Gordon** in 1684. A close adherent of James VII, who was deposed in

1688, Gordon became a Jacobite and suffered for it. For his constant flirtation with danger, and other more serious marital misdomenours, his wife, Elizabeth Howard, divorced Gordon in 1707. The Gordons continued his legacy of Jacobitism, although fought on both sides during the Jacobite risings of 1715 and 1745.

Alexander Gordon, second Duke of Gordon, 1678-1728, was a staunch Jacobite, and followed the standard of the 'Old Pretender' at the Battle of Sheriffmuir in 1715. He later surrendered, and was briefly imprisoned. His widow, Henrietta Mordaunt, ran the estate after her husband's death, and famously provided breakfast for Prince Charles Edward Stuart in 1745, a meal which led to her being punished by the government.

Cosmo George Gordon, the third Duke of Gordon, 1720-1752, remained loyal to the Hanoverians when Prince Charles Edward Stuart reasserted his father's claim in 1745, but his brother, Lord Louis Gordon, promptly deserted his post in the Royal Navy, returned to Scotland, and raised a regiment for the 'Bonnie Prince'. Cosmo was heavy-handed in his recruitment though, apparently imprisoning all those men on his family's lands who did not join him. After Culloden he escaped to France, where he died in 1754. Two further

Gordon regiments were raised, either voluntarily or through coercion, from the Duke's lands. Cosmo's forces came to about 800 men, although their quality and enthusiam varied wildly. Regardless, he secured a victory over the Government forces at the Battle of Inverurie on 23 December 1745, and his troops helped at the Jacobite victory at Falkirk. They suffered dreadfully at the Battle of Culloden, but retreated in good order, dispersing into the hills after the defeat.

Alexander Gordon, the fourth Duke of Gordon, 1743-1827, was also made the Duke of Huntley in the English peerage, Huntley being in Gloucester and having no connection with the Gordons. He is said to have created, popularised and standardised the Gordon Setter breed of dog. He also raised what would become the 92nd (Gordon Highlanders) Regiment of Foot in 1794, for service in the French Revolutionary Wars.

Scottish soldiers returning from the Napoleonic Wars

George, fifth Duke of Gordon, 1770-1836, was a general in the army and for a time governor of Edinburgh Castle. He served in Flanders, Corsica, Spain, Ireland and the Netherlands. A conservative to the bone, he opposed the 1832 Reform Act for electoral reform to the bitter end. He died without children, and the dukedom became extinct. Many of the Gordon treasures passed to the Brodies of Brodie, via the Duke's wife Elizabeth, where many can still be seen in Brodie Castle.

The marquessate passed to a kinsman, **George Gordon, fifth Earl of Aboyne** (1761–1853), who was descended from the second marquess. He became the ninth marquess and from him the present chiefs are descended.

The current chief of Clan Gordon is Granville Charles Gomer Gordon, thirteenth Marquess of Huntly, Earl of Enzie, Earl of Aboyne, Lord Gordon of Badenoch, Lord Gordon of Strathavon and Glenlivet, Baron Meldrum of Morven.

There are reputed to be some one-hundred-and-fifty-six branches of the Gordon kindred. It would be impossible to detail them all here, although it is worth pointing out some of the more remarkable ones.

GORDONS OF LOCHINVAR & KENMURE

The Gordons of Dumfries and Galloway descend from William, second son of Sir Adam Gordon (III) (active 1296-1309). Over time they came to dominate the stewartry of Kirkcudbright, at the expense of the Maxwells and the Douglasses, and were known for their hearty participation in cross-Border reiving, raiding in the north of England. John Gordon of Lochinvar was made Viscount of Kenmure by Charles I, but the power of the family was broken fighting for the Royalist side in the Wars of the Three Kingdoms in the 1640s. Unusually for the wider Gordons, the Gordons of Lochinvar were staunch Presbyterians rather than Catholic. William, the sixth viscount, 'the bravest lord that ever Galloway saw', rose for the Stuart cause in the 1715 Jacobite Rebellion, leading 150 cavalry in the invasion of England, but were defeated at Preston. As a result William was forfeited and executed. His widow, Mary Dalzell, managed to retrieve some of the confiscated family property at least.

Their original island castle of Lochinvar no longer survives, and the archaeological remains were submerged under the waters of the loch when it was dammed in the twentieth century to create a reservoir. A large square tower was reached by a submerged causeway in the water.

Kenmure Castle in the eighteenth century

The stately home of Kenmure Castle fell to decline after 1715, and was extensively remodelled in the nineteenth century when the family was restored. It was, however, unroofed in 1958 and now stands as a pathetic ruin, in need of some urgent care. A large sundial from the castle is now preserved in the musum of Dumfries.

THE GORDONS OF HADDO
& THE EARLS OF ABERDEEN

Haddo House in the nineteenth century

The Gordons of Haddo were a major cadet branch of the family, who descend from the late fourteenth-century Sir John Gordon. Important landowners in their own right, they were still powerful allies and supporters of the Earls of Huntly. Sir John Gordon of Haddo (1610-1644) was executed for his support of King Charles I during the Wars of the Three Kingdoms, having served with distinction under the Earl of Huntly. For the family's loyalty, Sir John's second son, George, was created Earl of Aberdeen in 1682.

The fourth earl was a Prime Minister of the United Kingdom from 1852 to 1855. Having played a key role in the diplomatic struggle against Napoleon 1812-1814, he became Foreign Secretary in 1828. He was central in bringing the Opium Wars to a close, a heavily one-sided affair where Britain and France devastated China, which saw the ceding of Hong Kong to Britain. As Prime Minister he led Britian, alongside France and the Ottoman Empire, in the Crimean War, against Russia, the mishandling of which bought down his govenment. He was also a scholar of Classical Civilisations, and a lover of Ancient Greek architecture.

The seventh earl, John Hamilton-Gordon, served as Lord-Liutenant of Ireland in 1886 and 1905 and was Govenor General of Canada, 1893 to 1898. His wife was the accomplished Ishbel Maria née Marjoribanks. Ishbel founded the 'Onwards and Upward Association', which sought to provide education to servant girls via postal instruction. She was also head of the Women's Liberal Federation, which sought to secure the right to vote for women. In 1931 she also headed a campaign to allow women to become ministers in the Kirk of Scotland, which was not achieved until 1969. Somewhat more successful was her introduction of the Golden Retriever to Canada, a breed of dog her father had devised.

THE GORDONS OF GIGHT

The Gight (pronounced 'Gecht') Gordons 'the most unruly family that ever reigned in Aberdeenshire', lived a little distance from their cousins at Haddo. Their castle of Gight still stands in ruins over the river Ythan and is now in the posession of the Haddo Gordons.

Through the sixteenth and seventeenth centuries the Gordons of Gight prooved themselves to be a quite violent and wild kindred, gleefully following their own bloodfeuds as well as those of the Earls of Huntly. The first laird, William Gordon of Gight was killed at Flodden in 1513. One of his sons was killed at Pinkie in 1547, and at other times three of his grandsons were murdered, another executed, another drowned and two more killed in battle. It was not uncommon for the Gights to duel, murder, or consequently, be murdered. As such, and combined with their Roman Catholicism, they often fell afoul of the Kirk and the Privy Council, although they seem to have rarely cared.

The last of their line was Catherine Gordon (d.1811). She was the mother of the famous poet Lord Byron, fittingly for a Gight, remembered as 'mad, bad and dangerous to know', who was partially raised at the dilapidated Gight Castle and the family's town house near Marischal College in Aberdeen. In later life he dropped the 'Gordon' in his name. Catherine sold Gight Castle to her Haddo cousins to service her husband's gambling debts. The Haddo Gordons used it for a time, but it was soon abandoned, leaving the ruin as we see it today.

George Gordon Byron

The Gordons of Cluny

The Gordons of Cluny descend from the second Earl of Huntly. They built a grand house at Cluny in 1603, which has got progressively grander over the centuries, the great house being one of the architectural gems of the north of Scotland. The main line of the Gordons of Cluny died out in the later eighteenth century.

The most notorious member of this family was John Gordon of Cluny (1776-1858). As a young man he served as a soldier, seeing action in Egypt, where he took the time to carve his name into a number of ancient monuments; some of his vandalism still being visible today. He inherited the Cluny estates in 1814. Prior to this, in 1801, he had inherited a huge fortune from his uncle, Alexander Gordon of Tobago, a slave plantation merchant, which left John a total of three major plantations with some 166 enslaved Africans, and a mortgage on another, which had 64 more enslaved souls. When slavery was abolished in 1834 John was compensated with £12,482. Such was his wealth, John was described as the richest commoner in Scotland. John was not the only member of this kindred to benefit fro the horrific system of chattel slavery. Some 210 Gordons have been recorded as having been associated with

Cluny Castle in about 1905

plantation slavery in the West Indies, many being compensated in 1834 when chattel slavery was abolished in most of the British Empire. Some Gordons owned as few as one soul, while others held whole plantations.

Sadly John didn't stop there. He purchased the islands of North and South Uist, Benbecula and Barra, from the impoverished chief of Clanranald in 1838 and he set about 'improving' these estates, turning the agricultural land over to sheep, which led to the forced expulsion of the people who had traditionally worked the lands on his islands. This was one of the most notorious episodes in the 'Highland Clearances'. In 1851 islanders were compelled to attend compulsory public meetings, where the unwitting islanders were then forced to board waiting ships to take them to Canada. Islanders attempting to flee were chased down with dogs.

John's line died with his illegitimate son John (who's mother was John's housekeeper), and the estates have passed sideways along the family to cousins since.

Conclusion

The history of every family is made up of good and bad, and this certainly applies to the Gordons. Throughout these pages we have seen a fair share of notorious characters (and occasionally utter monsters), but we have also seen better qualities occurring down the generations, with a strong quality of bravery and loyalty reoccurring. All men and women are shaped by their society, their circumstances and the turbulence of their times, and folk respond differently to these pressures, sometimes for the good, sometimes for the bad. What no one can dispute, however, is the centrality to the Gordons in Scottish history. Since Sir Adam Gordon delivered the declaration of Arbroth to the Pope in 1320, there is barely any event in Scotland's story that the Gordons weren't in some way or other a part of.

This brief history had provided a sketch of the story of the main lines of the Gordons – and, let's face it – focusing mostly on the nobles and aristocrats, and mostly men too, but it is hoped that members of the worldwide extended Gordon Kindred reading this will be able to place their own family stories into this outline, and will be keen to read more widely, and build themselves a richer picture of their illustrious ancestors.

THE GORDON HIGHLANDERS

The 92nd Regiment of Foot, the Gordon Highlanders were raised by the Duke of Gordon in 1794 (although numbered the 100th at the time), the majority of the men coming from his own estates and lured by promises of booty, and, more sinister assurances of security of tenure for the lands their families held from the duke: the implication being that if they didn't join they might be evicted. They were commanded by the Duke's son and heir, and soon prooved a brave and dependable force.

The regiment served throughout the French Revolutionary and Napoleonic Wars. Their most famous moment came at the Battle of Waterloo, where the Highlanders famously grabbed hold of the stirrups of the Scots Greys Cavalry, who were advancing to charge upon the French troops, to almighty cries of 'Scotland Forever!' In the nineteenth century the regiment served in Imperial missions in India, Afghanistan and South Africa. In 1881 the regiment absorbed the Stirlingshire Regiment, although retained the name of the Gordons. Further horrific fighting came in the First and Second World Wars. In 1994 the regiment merged with others to form the Highlanders Regiment, now, in turn, part of the Royal Regiment of Scotland.

Gordon Highlanders at Edinburgh Castle in 1842

FURTHER READING

The material for the introduction is based on the introductory chapters to George Way of Plean and Romilly Squire, *Scottish Clan & Family Encyclopaedia*, third Edition (2017), which is also available from St Kilda Publications. See that book for a fuller list of further reading for wider Scottish History and also for essential reading in Scottish history and introductions to the major clans and kindreds.

The early history of the Gordons is pieced together from the *People of Medieval Scotland 1093-1371* database, which can be searched here: www.poms.ac.uk

Much of the general history of the chiefly Gordon line can be found in volume 4 of Sir James Balfour Paul's *The Scots Peerage* (1907), which, despite its age, is still a thorough and detailed piece of research.

There are many books on the Gordons worth reading. The sixteenth and seventeenth centuries are especially well studied:

Harry Potter, *Bloodfeud: the Stewarts and Gordons at War* (2002)

Anne Forbes, *Trials and Triumphs, the Gordons of Huntly* (2012)

Barry Robertson, *Lordship and Power in the North of Scotland: The Noble House of Huntly 1603-1690* (2011)

The Gordon's involvement in the Transatlantic Slave Trade can be further researched via the *Legacies of British Slave-ownership* database, which can be found here: www.ucl.ac.uk/lbs

For the clan association, 'the House of Gordon', visit their website: www.houseofgordon.com

The USA association: www.houseofgordonusa.org

The Australian association: www.houseofgordon.net

GORDON TARTANS

The most well-known Gordon tartan (opposite, top), of blue and green base colours with a yellow stripe, was devised in 1793 by William Forsyth, a weaver of Huntly. He had been commissioned by the fourth Duke of Gordon, who wanted a pattern for the Gordon Highlanders Regiment. In essence, this tartan is based on the Black Watch regimental tartan, with the addition of the distinctive yellow stripe, which was added at the direction of the duke. Variants with two and three yellow stripes, also designed by Forsyth, were adopted by the cadet branches of the Gordon-Cummings of Altire and the Gordons of Esslemont respectively. Various Gordon tartans are then derived from this base, with the Ancient, Modern, Dress and Weathered versions.

The other major group of Gordon tartans come from the much older red Huntly District Tartan (opposite, bottom). District tartans were familiar sets known to a particular area in the days before 'clan' tartans. Variants of the Old Huntly tartan were worn by members of the Gordons, Brodies, Forbes, MacRaes, Munros and Rosses in the middle of the eighteenth century, and notably at the time of the 1745 Jacobite Rebellion. From this comes the grouping of 'Red Gordon' tartans.